Information Security based on ISO 27001/IS

MW00835463

Other publications by Van Haren Publishing

Van Haren Publishing (VHP) specializes in titles on Best Practices, methods and standards within four domains:
  - IT management,
  - Architecture (Enterprise and IT),
  - Business management and
  - Project management

These publications are grouped in series: *ITSM Library, Best Practice* and *IT Management Topics*. VHP is also publisher on behalf of leading companies and institutions:
The Open Group, IPMA-NL, PMI-NL, CA, Getronics, Quint, The Sox Institute and ASL BiSL Foundation

Topics are (per domain):

IT (Service) Management / IT Governance	Architecture (Enterprise and IT)	Project/Programme/ Risk Management
ASL	Archimate®	A4-Projectmanagement
BiSL	GEA®	ICB / NCB
CATS	TOGAF™	MINCE®
CMMI		M_o_R®
CobiT	**Business Management**	MSP
ISO 17799	EFQM	PMBoK®
ISO 27001	ISA-95	PRINCE2®
ISO/IEC 20000	ISO 9000	
ISPL	ISO 9001:2000	
IT Service CMM	SixSigma	
ITIL® V2	SOX	
ITIL® V3	SqEME®	
ITSM		
MOF		
MSF		
ABC of ICT		

For the latest information on VHP publications, visit our website: www.vanharen.net.

Information Security
based on
ISO 27001/ISO 27002
A Management Guide

Colophon

Title:	Information Security based on ISO 27001/ ISO 27002 - A Management Guide
Series:	Best Practice
Author:	Alan Calder
Chief Editor:	Jan van Bon
Publisher:	Van Haren Publishing, Zaltbommel, www.vanharen.net
ISBN:	978 90 8753 540 7
Edition:	First edition, first impression, May 2006 First edition, second impression, May 2008 Second edition, first impression, July 2009
Design and layout:	CO2 Premedia, Amersfoort-NL
Copyright:	© Van Haren Publishing, 2006, 2009
Printer:	Wilco, Amersfoort - NL

This title was updated in 2009 to reflect changes made to the Standard in 2008.

Permission to reproduce extracts of BS ISO/IEC 27001: 2005 (BS 7799-2: 2005) is granted by BSI. British Standards can be obtained from BSI Customer Services, 389 Chiswick High Road, London W4 4AL. Tel: +44 (0)20 8996 9001.
email: cservices@bsi-global.com

For any further enquiries about Van Haren Publishing, please send an e-mail to:
info@vanharen.net

Aknowledgements

Van Haren Publishing would like to thank Alan Calder, the lead author, for his expert, flexible approach and his professional delivery.

Title: Information Security based on ISO 27001/ ISO 27002 -
                A Management Guide

Lead Author: Alan Calder

Editors: Jan van Bon (Inform-IT), Chief Editor
                Selma Polter, Editor

Review Team: Dr Gary Hinson   IsecT
                Steve G Watkins,   HMCPSI (UK Government:
                                   Crown Prosecution Service Inspectorate)
                Dr Jon G. Hall   Centre for Research in Computing,
                                   The Open University

Contents

CHAPTER 1

Introduction

This Management Guide provides an overview of the two international information security standards, ISO/IEC 27001:2005 and ISO/IEC 27002:2005.

It provides an introduction and overview to both the Standards. It is not a substitute for acquiring (from national standards bodies or licensed online resellers) and reading the Standards themselves. This book briefly describes the background to the current version of the Standards. It also looks briefly at links to other standards, such as *ISO 9001, BS25999* and *ISO 20000*, and to frameworks such as *CobiT* and *ITIL*. Above all, it describes how ISO 27001 and ISO 27002 interact to guide organizations in the development of best practice information security management systems.

1.1   Originating body: ISO/IEC JTC1/SC 27

ISO (the International Organization for Standardization) and IEC (the International Electrotechnical Commission) have established a joint technical committee, ISO/IEC JTC 1, to deal with their mutual interest in the field of information technology. This committee has a number of sub-committees; one of these, SC 27, is responsible for IT security techniques. This committee is responsible for producing both the Standards described in this Management Guide.

1.2   ISO/IEC 27001:2005 ('ISO 27001' or 'the Standard')

This is the most recent, most up-to-date, international version of a standard specification for an Information Security Management System. It is vendor-neutral and technology-independent. It is designed for use in organizations of all sizes ('intended to be applicable to all organizations, regardless of type, size and nature'[1]) and in every sector (e.g. 'commercial enterprises, government agencies, not-for-profit organizations'[2]), anywhere in the world. It is a management system, not a technology specification and this is reflected in its formal title, which is 'Information Technology - Security Techniques - Information Security Management Systems - Requirements.' ISO 27001 is also the first of a series of international information security standards, all of which will have ISO 27000 numbers.

1.3   ISO/IEC 27002:2005 ('ISO 27002')

This Standard is titled 'Information Technology - Security Techniques - Code of Practice for information security management.' Published in July 2005, it replaced ISO/.IEC 17799:2000, which has now been withdrawn. While it was initially numbered ISO/IEC 17799, this standard has also been given the number ISO/IEC 27002 number in order to make it a member of the ISO27000 series of standards.

1.4   Definitions

The definitions used in both Standards are intended to be consistent with one another and also to be consistent with those used in related information security standards, such as ISO/IEC Guide 73:2002, ISO/IEC 13335-1:2004, etc.

---

1) ISO/IEC 27001:2005 Application 1.2

2) ISO/IEC 27001:2005 Scope 1.1

CHAPTER 2

Information security

It is a truism to say that information is the currency of the information age. Information is, in many cases, the most valuable asset possessed by an organization, even if that information has not been subject to a formal and comprehensive valuation.

IT governance is the discipline that deals with the structures, standards and processes that boards and management teams apply to effectively manage, protect and exploit their organization's information assets.

Information security management is that subset of IT governance that focuses on protecting and securing an organization's information assets.

2.1 Risks to information assets

An asset is defined in ISO 27001 as 'anything that has value to an organization'. Information assets are subject to a wide range of threats, both external and internal, ranging from the random to the highly specific. Risks include acts of nature, fraud and other criminal activity, user error and system failure. Information risks can affect one or more of the three fundamental attributes of an information asset: its:

- availability;
- confidentiality;
- integrity.

These three attributes are defined in ISO 27001 as follows:

- *availability* - 'the property of being accessible and usable upon demand by an authorized entity', which allows for the possibility that information has to be accessed by software programs as well as human users;
- *confidentiality* - 'the property that information is not made available or disclosed to unauthorized individuals, entities, or processes';
- *integrity* - 'the property of safeguarding the accuracy and completeness of assets'.

2.2   Information security

ISO 27001 defines information security as the 'preservation of confidentiality, integrity and availability of information; in addition, other properties such as authenticity, accountability, non-repudiation and reliability can also be involved.'

2.3   Information Security Management System

ISO 27001 defines an ISMS, or Information Security Management System, as 'that part of the overall management system, based on a business risk approach, to establish, implement, operate, monitor, review, maintain and improve information security. The management system includes organizational structure, policies, planning activities, responsibilities, practices, procedures, processes and resources.' An ISMS exists to preserve confidentiality, integrity and availability. As figure 2.1 shows, the ISMS secures the confidentiality, availability and integrity of the organization's information and information assets, and its most critical information assets are those for which all three attributes are important.

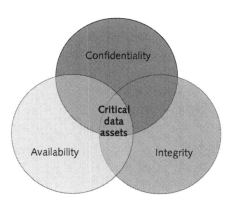

Figure 2.1 *Attributes of Information Assets*

CHAPTER 3

Background to the Standards

The information security standard, BS7799, was first issued in April 1999, as a two-part standard. An earlier Code of Practice had been substantially revised and became Part 1 of the new standard (BS7799-1:1999) and a new Part 2 (BS7799-2:1999) was drafted and added.

Part 1 was titled 'Code of Practice for Information Security Management' and it provided guidance on best practice in information security management. Its foreword clearly stated that it was not to be treated as a specification.

Part 2, titled 'Specification for Information Security Management Systems,' was drafted as the specification against which an organization's security management system could be assessed and certificated.

The link between the two Standards was, from the outset, through Annex A of BS7799-2, which lists all the information security controls whose applicability organizations are required to consider. This list of controls is aligned with the controls of BS7799-1, and BS7799-2 requires the user to seek more detailed guidance on how to implement the listed controls from BS7799-1.

3.1 First certification

The first organization in the world to have its ISMS certified as being in conformance with BS7799-2:1999 was Business Link London City Partners. Since then, there have been nearly two thousand certifications; by December 2008, there were over 7,000 certifications.

3.2 ISO 17799:2000

BS7799-1:1999 began to be adopted by other national standards bodies becoming, for instance, AS 4444 in Australia and NZS 4444 in New Zealand. The International Standards Organization (ISO) and the International Electrotechnical Commission

(IEC)[3] then collaborated to adopt and internationalize BS7799-1 as ISO/IEC 17799:2000 in December 2000.

This version of the Guidelines was dual numbered in some countries so that, for example, in the UK it was numbered BS7799-1:2000 (ISO/IEC 17799:2000). It was exactly the same document, whatever number it was given.

ISO 17799 was substantially revised, improved and updated five years later and, as ISO/IEC 17799:2005 it was far more in line with today's information security requirements. In the course of 2008, it was given the number ISO/IEC 27002:2005, in order to clearly tie it into the ISO/IEC 27000 series of information security management standards.

3.3 BS7799-2

BS7799-2:1999 was revised in 2002 and re-issued as BS7799-2:2002. The significant changes that occurred at this time included:
- the alignment of the clause numbering in both parts of the Standard;
- the addition of the PDCA model (see Chapter 15) to the Standard;
- the addition of a requirement to continuously improve the ISMS;
- the alignment of the Standard, and its detailed clauses, with ISO 9001:2000 and ISO 14001:1996, to facilitate the development of integrated management systems.

3.4 International adoption

BS7799-2:2002 was then adopted by the national standards bodies in a number of countries including Brazil, the Czech Republic, Finland, Iceland, Ireland, the Netherlands, Norway and Sweden and issued by them as their own national standards. For instance, the Australian and New Zealand standards bodies (Standards Australia and Standards New Zealand) jointly issued in 2003 a local version of BS7799-2:2002 under the number AS/NZS 7799.2.2003. Similarly, it was accepted by the South African Bureau of Standards as SABS 7799/2, in April 2002, while Spain developed its own version, UNE 71502:2004.

---

3) The IEC is 'the leading global organization that prepares and publishes international standards for all electrical, electronic and related technologies.' Its website is at www.iec.ch. The ISO and the IEC work together, within the World Trade Organization (WTO) framework, to provide technical support for the growth of global markets and to ensure that technical regulations, voluntary standards and conformity assessment procedures do not create unnecessary obstacles to trade. The joint ISO/IEC information centre has a website at www.standardsinfo.net/isoiec/index.html.

3.5 Translations and sector schemes

The Standard has also been translated into a number of languages, including Chinese, Czech, Danish, Dutch, Finnish, French, German, Icelandic, Japanese, Korean, Norwegian, Portuguese and Swedish. At the same time, a number of sector schemes have been developed. These are versions of BS7799-2:2002 that have been adapted and amended for specific sectors, such as the APACS Standard 55, the information security management standard now mandated by the UK payment services association for all its members.

3.6 ISO 27001:2005

BS7799-2 was still only a British Standard in June 2005, when ISO 17799:2005 was issued. The decision was taken, at that time, to put it on the 'fast track' to internationalization and FDIS (Final Draft International Standard) was issued in June 2005. BS7799-2:2005 (ISO/IEC 27001:2005) was finally published in October 2005.

It 'can be used to assess conformance by interested internal and external parties.' It is the specific document against which an ISMS can be assessed.

ISO/IEC 27001:2005 and ISO/IEC 27002:2005 still have the symbiotic relationship of a two-part standard.

CHAPTER 4

Relationship between the Standards

The working relationship between ISO 27001 and ISO 27002 needs to be very clear, as ISO 27001 relies to such a substantial extent on ISO 27002 that it in effect mandates use of ISO 27002.

The link between the two Standards was created in 1999, when BS7799 was first published as a two part standard:

- Part 1 was a Code of Practice;
- Part 2 was a specification for an ISMS that deployed controls selected from the Code of Practice.

The original Part 2 specified, in the main body of the Standard, the same set of controls that were described, in far greater detail (particularly with regard to implementation) in Part 1. These controls were later removed from the main body of Part 2 and listed in an annex, Annex A.

This relationship continues today, between the specification for the ISMS that is contained in one part of the combined Standard, and the detailed guidance on the information security controls that should be considered in developing and implementing the ISMS and which are contained in the other part of the combined Standard. The planned addition of further standards in the ISO 2700x series is not expected to change this fundamental relationship between ISO 27001 and ISO 27002.

4.1 Why develop an international code of practice?

The reason for developing ISO 27002 as an international standard for information security management was originally described by BSI on their website as follows:

Many organizations have expressed the need to have a common standard on best practice for information security management. They would like to be able to implement information security controls to meet their own business requirements as well as a set of controls for their business relationships with other organizations. These organizations see the need to share the benefits of common best practice at a true international level to ensure that they can protect their business processes and activities to satisfy these business needs. (BSI-DISC website)

The ISO/IEC 17799:2000 Code of Practice was intended to provide a framework for international best practice in Information Security Management and systems interoperability. It also provided guidance on how to implement an ISMS that would be capable of certification, and to which an external auditor could refer.

It did not provide the basis for an international certification scheme. Only BS7799-2 - and now ISO 27001 - can do that.

4.2 Correspondence between the two Standards

Annex A to ISO/IEC 27001:2005 lists the 133 controls that are in ISO/IEC 17799:2005, follows the same numbering system and uses the same words for those controls.

The preface to ISO 27001 states: 'The control objectives and controls referred to in this edition are directly derived from and aligned with those listed in ISO/IEC 17799:2005.' ISO/IEC 27001 requires that 'control objectives and controls from Annex A shall be selected' in order to meet the 'requirements identified by the risk assessment and risk treatment process.'

ISO 27002 also provides substantial implementation guidance on how individual controls should be approached. Anyone implementing an ISO 27001 ISMS will need to acquire and study copies of both ISO 27001 and ISO 27002.

While ISO 27001 mandates the use of ISO 27002 as a source of guidance on controls, control selection and control implementation, it does not limit the organization's choice of controls. The preface goes on to state: 'The list of control objectives and controls in this ISO Standard is not exhaustive and an organization might consider that additional control objectives and controls are necessary.'[4]

---

4) ISO/IEC 27001:2005 Preface

CHAPTER 5

Use of the Standards

Both Standards recognize that information security cannot be achieved through technological means alone, and should never be implemented in a way that is either out of line with the organization's approach to risk or which undermines or creates difficulties for its business operations.

Effective information security is defined in both ISO 27001 and ISO 27002 as the 'preservation of confidentiality, integrity and availability of information'.

5.1   Specification compared to a Code of Practice

ISO/IEC 27001:2005 is a specification for an ISMS. It uses words like '*shall*'. It sets out requirements.

A Code of Practice or a set of guidelines uses words like '*should*' and '*may*', allowing individual organizations to choose which elements of the Standard to implement, and which not. ISO 27001 does not provide any such latitude.

Any organization that implements an ISMS which it wishes to have assessed against the Standard will have to follow the specification contained in the Standard.

As a general rule, organizations implementing an ISMS based on ISO/IEC 27001:2005 will do well to pay close attention to the wording of the Standard itself, and to be aware of any revisions to it. Non-compliance with any official revisions, which usually occur on a three-year and a five-year cycle, will jeopardize an existing certification.

ISO 27001 itself is what an ISMS will be assessed against; where there is any conflict between advice provided in this or any other guide to implementation of ISO 27001 and the Standard itself, it is the wording in the Standard that should be heeded.

An external certification auditor assesses the ISMS against the published Standard, not against the advice provided by this book, a sector scheme manager, a consultant or any other third party. It is critical that those responsible for the ISMS should be able to refer explicitly to its clauses and intent and should be able to defend any implementation steps they have taken against the Standard itself.

An appropriate first step is to obtain and read a copy of ISO/IEC 27001:2005. Copies can be purchased from the ISO website, from national standards bodies and from www. itgovernance.co.uk. There should be a choice of hard copy and downloadable versions to suit individual needs.

5.2   The ISMS

An ISMS - which the Standard is clear includes 'organizational structure, policies, planning activities, responsibilities, practices, procedures, processes and resources,'[5] - is a structured, coherent management approach to information security which is designed to ensure the effective interaction of the three key components of implementing an information security policy:

- process (or procedure);
- technology;
- user behavior.

The Standard's requirement is that the design and implementation of an ISMS should be directly influenced by each organization's 'needs and objectives, security requirements, the processes employed and the size and structure of the organization.'[6]
ISO 27001 is not a one size-fits-all solution, nor was it ever seen as a static, fixed entity that interferes with the growth and development of the business. The Standard explicitly recognizes that:

- the ISMS 'will be scaled in accordance with the needs of the organization';
- a 'simple situation requires a simple ISMS solution';
- the ISMS is 'expected to change over time.'

5.3   ISO 27001 as a model for the ISMS

In the simple terms of the Standard, it is a useful model for 'establishing, implementing, operating, monitoring, reviewing, maintaining and improving an ISMS.'[7] It is a model that can be applied anywhere in the world, and understood anywhere in the world. It is consistent, coherent, contains the assembled best practice, experience and expertise gathered from implementations throughout the world over the last ten years, and it is technology-neutral. It is designed for implementation in any hardware or software environment.
It should be noted that having an ISO 27001-compliant ISMS will not automatically 'in itself confer immunity from legal obligations.'[8] The organization will have to ensure that it understands the range of legislation and regulation with which it must comply, and ensure that these requirements are reflected in their ISMS.

---

5) ISO/IEC 27001:2005 Terms and Definitions 3.7 Note
6) ISO/IEC 27001:2005 Introduction General 0.1
7) All four quotes from ISO/IEC 27001:2005 Introduction General 0.1
8) ISO/IEC 27001:2005 Title Note

CHAPTER 6

Certification process and certification bodies

ISO 27001 provides a specification against which an organization's ISMS can be independently audited by an accredited certification body. If the ISMS is found to conform to the specification, the organization can be issued with a formal certificate confirming this.

6.1 Certification bodies

Certification is carried out by independent, accredited certification bodies. These have different names in different countries, including 'registration bodies', 'assessment and registration bodies', 'certification/registration bodies' and 'registrars'. Whatever they are called, they all do the same thing and are subject to the same requirements.
An accredited certification body is one that has demonstrated to a national accreditation body (such as, for example, UKAS - the UK Accreditation Service) that it has fully met the international and any national standards set down for the operation of certification bodies.

6.2 Standards for certification bodies

In the context of the ISMS, these Standards include:
* ISO/IEC 27006:2007 (Information technology - Security techniques - Requirements for bodies providing audit and certification of information security management systems);
* the accreditation guidelines EA 7/03. EA 7/03 (European cooperation for Accreditation) 7/03 are the specific guidelines for the accreditation of bodies operating certification or registration of information security management systems, and were drawn largely from ISO/IEC Guide 62, together with additional guidance material. ISO/IEC 17021:2006, which is titled: 'Conformity assessment - requirements for bodies providing audit and certification of management systems.'

ISO/IEC 17021, which sets out the requirements for how accredited certification bodies should operate, states clearly that neither audit team members nor their organization can provide consulting services to any organization that they are certifying. As a consequence, certification bodies tend to limit their activities to certification audits and public (i.e. no client on-site) training.

Organizations that are seeking independent certification of their ISMS should always go to an accredited certification body. Their certificates are usually valid for three years and are subject to periodic maintenance visits by the certification body; they have international credibility and will be issued in line with an approved system for the issue and maintenance of such certificates. There is a short list of some accredited certification and other bodies in Appendix 2 of this guide.

In the UK, the United Kingdom Accreditation Service (UKAS) operates under a Memorandum of Understanding from the Department of Trade and Industry. UKAS accredits the competence of certification bodies - both inside and outside the UK - to perform services in the areas of product and management system approval. The UK's ISO 27001 Accredited Certification Scheme was originally launched in April 1998.

6.3 The certification process

The certification process will be completely familiar to any organization that has already undergone certification to ISO 9000 or any other management system standard.

The certification body will want to go through an initial two-stage process. The first stage will be a documentation review (which may, or may not, include a pre-certification visit), and this enables the auditors who will carry out the actual formal initial visit to:

- become acquainted with the organization
- carry out a document review
- assure themselves that the ISMS is sufficiently well developed to be capable of withstanding a formal audit
- obtain enough information about the organization and the intended scope of the certification to effectively plan their audit.

This visit is usually relatively short and, depending on the size of the organization, may require only one or two days to carry out. Some organizations will carry out the document review remotely, before making a visit.

6.4   The formal audit

The formal audit, usually known as the 'Initial Visit', will take place over a number of days. The audit process involves testing the organization's documented processes (the ISMS) against the requirements of the Standard, to confirm that the organization has set out to comply with the Standard, and then testing actual compliance by the organization with its ISMS.

The audit will follow a pre-ordained plan. The auditors will have communicated with whoever is their liaison point at the organization about who they will wish to interview and in what order they will want to do it.

6.5   The audit report

A certification audit will use negative reporting (i.e. it will identify inadequacies, rather than adequacies) to assess an ISMS to ensure that its documented procedures and processes, the actual activities of the organization and the records of implementation meet the requirements of ISO 27001 and the declared scope of the system. The outcome of the audit will be:

- a written audit report (usually available at completion of the audit)
- a number of non-conformances and observations
- agreed corrective actions and time frames.

Non-conformances can be either minor or major; minor ones should be seen as improvement opportunities and major ones will mean the organization is not (at this stage) capable of successful certification. Often, upon identification of a major non-conformance, the auditors will suggest that the audit process be suspended and started afresh once the organization has had time enough to resolve this major issue.

6.6   Outcome of the audit

The expected outcome of the initial visit should be certification of the ISMS to ISO 27001 and the issue of a certificate to this effect. The certificate should be appropriately displayed and the organization should start preparing for its first surveillance visit, which will take place in about six months' time.

Any minor non-conformances should be capable of being resolved by mail and any certificate issued will be dependent on this happening within an agreed timescale.

Audit observations should be addressed during the post-audit phase, both to ensure that they don't develop into non-conformances and as part of the organization's continuous improvement activity.

An approved version of the scheme certification symbol may be used in the organization's marketing material.

CHAPTER 7

Overview of ISO 27001

This Standard's title is 'Information Technology - Security Techniques - Information Security Management Systems - Requirements'. From October 2005, it replaced BS7799-2:2002, which was withdrawn. In the United Kingdom, it is dual-numbered, as BS7799-2:2005.

Including end pieces, this Standard is only 44 pages long. The core of the Standard is contained in the nine pages that set out the specifications for the design and implementation of an Information Security Management System, and in the 17 pages of Annex A, which contain the 133 individual controls which, must under the Standard, be considered for applicability.

The ISMS specification is contained in clauses four to eight of ISO 27001, and each of them is discussed further in this Management Guide.

The Standard's contents (main clauses and annexes) are:
* Introduction
* Scope
* Normative references
* Terms and definitions
* Information Security Management System
* Management responsibility
* Internal ISMS audits
* Management review of the ISMS
* ISMS Improvement
* Annex A Control objectives and controls
* Annex B OECD Principals and this international standard
* Annex C Correspondence between ISO 9001:2000, ISO14001:2004 and this international standard
* Bibliography

7.1 Main clauses

The main clauses of ISO 27001 (together with the chapters of this Management Guide in which they are covered) are:
* 4.1 General requirements
* Establish the ISMS (Chapters 16 to 20)

- Implement and operate the ISMS (Chapter 21)
- Monitor and review the ISMS (Chapter 22)
- Maintain and improve the ISMS (Chapter 23)
- Documentation requirements (Chapter 13)
- General
- Control of documents
- Control of records
- Management responsibility (Chapter 14)
- Management commitment
- Resource management
- Provision of resources
- Training, awareness and competence
- Internal ISMS audits (Chapter 22)
- Management review of the ISMS (Chapter 22)
- General
- Review Input
- Review Output
- ISMS improvement (Chapter 23)
- Continual improvement
- Corrective action
- Preventive action

7.2 ISMS building blocks: relationship between ISO/IEC 27001 Clauses 4-8, ISO/IEC 27001 Annex A, and ISO/IEC 27002

The Clause 4 general requirements of ISO/IEC 27001 are underpinned by the specific requirements of Clauses 5 through to 8. The list of controls contained in Annex A directly correlates to the detailed guidance contained in ISO/IEC 27002, and it is these controls that form the bulk of the ISMS. Figure 7.1 shows these building blocks.

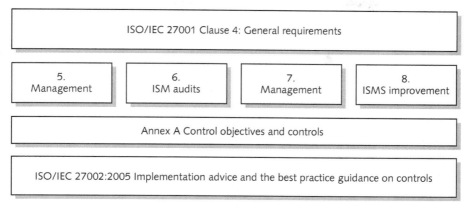

Figure 7.1 *Relationship between ISO/IEC 27001 Clause 4 and Annex A*

7.3   General requirements

While all these clauses are important, the one that initially has the most bearing on the effectiveness or otherwise of the ISMS is Clause 4.2.1: Establish the ISMS.
Clause 4.2.1 deals with six critical items:

- scope - the definition of the organization to which the ISMS applies, and which is discussed further in Chapter 16
- policy - the board's information security policy, which sets the guidelines for the whole ISMS, and which is discussed further in Chapter 17
- asset inventory - the information assets, of all types (tangible and intangible) which are to be the subject of the ISMS, and which is discussed further in Chapter 18
- risk assessment - the identification of the risks that relate to each asset, and which is also discussed further in Chapter 18
- risk treatment plan - identification of how each risk is to be dealt with, within the context of the board's overall approach to risk, and which is discussed further in Chapter 19
- Statement of Applicability - which describes which of the controls in Annex A of ISO 27001 have been applied, and how, and which have not been applied, together with a justification for their exclusion, and which is discussed further in Chapter 20.

7.4   Other content

The rest of the Standard consists of:
*   introductory material
*   definitions (which should be applied throughout the ISMS)
*   the process approach (which is discussed further in Chapter 15)
*   two informative (i.e. not mandatory) annexes: B, which identifies correspondences between the contents of ISO 27001
*   the OECD Guidelines for the Security of Information Systems and Networks
*   Annex C, which identifies clause-by-clause correspondences between ISO 27001, ISO 9001 and ISO 14001 (further discussed in Chapter 12).

CHAPTER 8

Summary of changes from BS7799-2:2002

The changes that have been made to BS7799-2:2002 as part of its internationalization are relatively minor, in comparison to those made to ISO 27002. This chapter is really only for those who are already familiar with BS7799-2:2002 and are interested in an overview of the changes that were introduced at internationalization or who have to update an existing ISMS to meet the requirements of ISO 27001.

Clause numbering is virtually unchanged, except at the back end of the Standard, where Clauses 6.1, 6.2 and 6.3 have been re-numbered in order to allow what was a sub-clause of 6 (Clause 6.4, Internal ISMS Audits) to be elevated to a new, first level Clause 6. This demonstrates the importance of effective internal audit, in the overall context of the ISMS.

8.1 Greater clarity in specifications

All the other changes are designed to provide greater clarity in the specification of the ISMS; the most significant ones are listed below:

- 1.2 - this clause now makes it clear that exclusions from Clauses 4-8 of the Standard will not be acceptable, but that under certain specified conditions exclusions from the control requirements of Annex A may be.
- 4.2.1a) - this clause now requires that any exclusions from the scope of the ISMS be justified and that its boundaries be identified.
- 1.2.1 c) - this clause has been varied to stress that the organization's approach to risk assessment must be systematic, although it is difficult to imagine the point of an unsystematic approach
- 4.2.1 g) - this clause has been extended to include a requirement that control selection should take account of the organization's risk acceptance criteria as well as legal, regulatory and any contractual requirements.
- 4.2.2 d) - this is an additional requirement and it is a mark of the growing requirement for an ISMS to include methods of measuring the effectiveness of controls and groups of controls, and for specifying how these measures are to be used to ensure that control effectiveness is maintained. The fact that a new standard, to deal with

ISMS measurements, is being developed should come as a surprise to no one. The requirement for greater measurement appears in the revisions to :

- 4.2.3 a) 'execute monitoring and review procedures and other controls to detect security events'
- 4.2.3 c) 'measure the effectiveness of controls'
- the requirement in 7.2 f) to review 'results from effectiveness measurements'
- the requirement in 7.3 e) to review output that includes a review of the 'improvement to how the effectiveness of controls is being measured'.

Other changes include clarification that:

- a description of the risk assessment methodology must be provided (4.3.1 d)
- documents must be available (4.3.2 f)
- some significant changes to the documentation requirements of Clause 4.3.1, all of which are touched upon in Chapter 13.

CHAPTER 9

Overview of ISO 27002:2005

This Standard's title is 'Information Technology - Security Techniques - Code of Practice for information security management'. Published in July 2005, it replaced ISO/.IEC 17799:2000, which has now been withdrawn. In the United Kingdom, it is dual-numbered BS7799-1:2005. From 2008, this Standard has been renumbered (without any changes) as ISO/IEC 27002 :2005.

It is a Code of Practice, not a specification. It uses words like 'should' and 'may'. It 'may serve as a practical guideline for developing organizational security standards and effective security management practices and help build confidence in inter-organizational activities.'[9]

ISO 27002:2005 is nearly three times longer than ISO 27001, with 126 pages, 11 of which are introductory material. 96 pages deal, in detail with information security controls. This Standard has 15 clauses, as shown below:

- Foreword
1. Introduction
2. Scope
3. Terms and definitions
4. Structure of the Standard
5. Risk assessment and treatment
6. Security policy
7. Organization of information security
8. Asset management
9. Human resources security
10. Physical and environmental security
11. Communications and operations management
12. Access control
13. Information systems acquisition, development and maintenance
14. Information security incident management
15. Business continuity management
16. Compliance
- Bibliography
- Index

---

9) ISO/IEC 27002:2005, 1 Scope

The eleven clauses numbered from five to fifteen contain the controls that are specified in Annex A of ISO 27001. These clauses collectively contain 39 security categories. The numbering of the controls is exactly the same in both Standards. There is no significance to the order of the clauses; 'depending on the circumstances, all clauses could be important.'[10]

9.1   The security categories

Each security category contains:
- a control objective, stating what has to be achieved
- one or more controls that can be deployed to achieve that stated objective.

Each control within each security category is laid out in exactly the same way. There is:
- a control statement, which describes (in the context of the control objective) what the control is for
- implementation guidance, which is detailed guidance which may (or may not) help individual organizations implement the control
- other information that needs to be considered, including reference to other standards.

9.2   ISMS building blocks: relationship between the control clauses of ISO/IEC 27002:2005

As figure 9.1 illustrates, the ISMS policy is the apex of the ISMS; all its other components are subsidiary. Policy is owned by top management and those building blocks that are furthest removed from the policy are those with which top management has least direct involvement. They are all operational responsibilities.

---

10) ISO/IEC 27002:2005, Note to claus 3.1

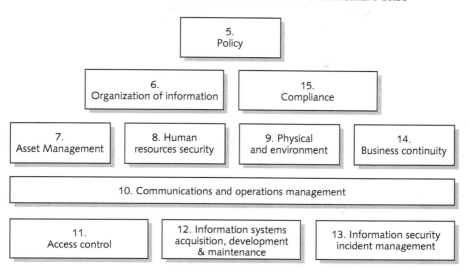

Figure 9.1 *Relationship between the control clauses of ISO/IEC 27002:2005*

CHAPTER 10

Summary of changes from ISO 27002:2000

ISO 17799:2000 was very substantially revised during 2005, in line with the normal ISO cycle of performing major reviews and updates of international standards on a five-yearly cycle.

10.1 Clause changes

12 clauses were increased to 15:

- one new clause (Clause 3) explained the structure of the Standard, but has no real impact on the deployment of an ISMS
- the second new clause (Clause 4, 'Risk Assessment and Treatment') was taken from the introduction to the previous version of the Standard. This clause is important because ISO 27002 now reflects, as guidance, the ISO 27001 requirement that that selection of control objectives and controls should be made in the light of (a) risk assessment(s)
- all the clauses around Information Security Incident Management were now consolidated into the third of the new clauses, clause 13.

There are 39 security categories, each of which has a control objective.

10.2 Layout of controls

The way in which controls were laid out was changed; each control within each security category was laid out in exactly the same way. There is:

- a control statement, which describes (in the context of the control objective) what the control is for
- implementation guidance, which is detailed guidance which may (or may not) help individual organizations implement the control
- other information that needs to be considered, including reference to other standards.

10.3 Control changes

36 control areas and controls in ISO 27002:2000 have been deleted, or re-structured and moved to somewhere else in the Standard.

46 new control areas and controls have been added, which includes those that were deleted from elsewhere in the Standard, re-structured and re-inserted.

All the remaining controls have changes, ranging from minor (e.g. wording adjustments to bring the control into line with the new format for controls) to major re-structuring. These changes are too extensive to be usefully described in a Management Guide. Readers are encouraged to obtain a commercial standards conversion tool if they need detailed, side-by-side comparison of the two Standards.

CHAPTER 11

ISO 27000 series in future

The International Standards Organization, working through a sub-committee identified as ISO/IEC JTC 1/SC 27 WG1, is launching a series of information security standards that are modeled on the ISO 9000 series concept.

11.1 ISO 27001

The first of these to be released, in October 2005, was ISO/IEC 27001:2005, the Standard which replaced BS7799-2:2002 (this was withdrawn on publication of ISO 27001). This is titled 'Information technology - Security Techniques - Information Security Management Systems - Requirements.'

11.2 ISO 27002

This was followed, in 2008, with ISO/IEC 27002, which replaced ISO/IEC 17799:2005. At a stroke, it simplified everyone's understanding of how the two Standards relate to one another.

11.3 ISO 27003

This number has been reserved for a Code of Practice which is intended to provide guidance on the implementation of an ISMS that conforms to ISO27001.

11.4 ISO 27004

A new third part of the Standard, ISO/IEC 27004, with the provisional title 'Information Security Metrics and Measurement', is actively being developed; there is not yet a launch date. This Standard will help organizations more effectively address the requirement, contained in Clauses 7.2 and 7.3 of ISO 27001, to measure the effectiveness of controls.

ISO/IEC 27005:2008, titled 'Information technology - Security techniques - Information security risk management' is a Code of Practice that provides guidance on risk assessment for ISO27001. Risk Assessment is a core competence of the Standard.

11.5 ISO/IEC 27005:2008

ISO/IEC 27005:2008, titled 'Information technology - Security techniques - Information security risk management' is a Code of Practice that provides guidance on risk assessment for ISO27001. Risk Assessment is a core competence of the Standard.

CHAPTER 12

Compatibility and integration with other management systems

BS7799-2:2002 contained the first formal attempt to harmonies the ISMS standard with ISO 9001:2000 and ISO 14001:1996. This step reflected the attempts made by a number of organizations to integrate and align their management systems - including Business Link London City Partners, the first organization ever to achieve BS7799-2 certification, which also created the world's first completely integrated management system that achieved certification to BS7799-2, ISO 9001 and ISO 14001.

12.1 ISO 27001 Annex C and integration

Annex C to ISO 27001 is informative, not mandatory - no organization is required to try and integrate its management systems. This Annex shows how its individual clauses correspond to the clauses of ISO 9001:2008 and ISO 14001:2004. For most, but not all, organizations, the critical correspondences will be between ISO 27001 and ISO 9001. The following ISO 27001 clauses are the starting point for management system integration:

- Clause 4.3, which deals with documentation requirements
- Clauses 5.1, which deal with management commitment
- Clause 7, which deals with management review
- Clause 6, which deals with internal audits.

These clauses, between them, make possible the deployment of common documentation, management and audit processes for both management systems.

12.2 The integrated management system

An integrated management system only needs:

- a single manual that incorporates its quality and its information security procedures
- a single comprehensive and integrated audit process that covers all aspects of its activity

- a standard management authorization, approval, monitoring and review process that deals with all its activities irrespective of whether they fall within the scope of the information security management system, the quality management system or the environmental management system.

12.3 ISO 9001

Organizations that already have an ISO 9001-compliant system in place can simply extend it to include an ISMS that will be capable of certification to ISO 27001. The note to Clause 1.2 recognizes this:

'If an organization already has an operative business process management system, it is preferable in most cases to satisfy the requirements of this International Standard within this existing management system.'

12.4 BS25999

BS25999 provides a specification for a business continuity management framework that can make a significant contribution to the development of the business continuity plan(s) that are specified as being required in Clause A. 14 of the Annex to ISO 27001. This is appropriate for medium and large organizations certainly, and often for smaller ones. This clause of the Standard pre-supposes the existence of such a plan and focuses only on the information security aspects of that plan.

This means that organizations must look outside ISO 27001 and ISO 27002 for guidance on the development of their business continuity framework and plans. The only formal standard to which they can turn is BS25999 and it makes practical sense for an organization to seek guidance on such a mission-critical subject from a standard such as this. Copies of BS25999 can be obtained from BSI and from other standards distributors. BS25999 uses terms that will be familiar to those developing an ISMS, including 'risk assessment' and 'impacts'. The principle that ought to be applied is that, where there is any gap between the requirements of ISO 27001 (including in definitions, process, etc) and the guidance of BS25999, it is ISO 27001 that must have primacy, if accredited certification is being sought.

A business continuity framework developed in line with BS25999 will certainly be adequate to the requirements of an information security management system and will be capable of supporting the control requirements of ISO 27001's A.14.

CHAPTER 13

Documentation requirements and record control

One of the key reasons for designing and implementing a management system is to enable the organization to move beyond what is known, in Capability Maturity Model terms, as an 'ad-hoc' organization. An ad-hoc organization is one that has 'no fixed processes, or procedures, results depend very much on individual performance, and a lot of people's time is spent on 'firefighting', fixing bugs in software, and resolving incidents.'[11]

ISO 9001:2008 is a well known and widely implemented quality assurance or business process management system. If the organization does not already have an existing ISO 9001 certified management system and needs guidance on the documentation, document control and records issues covered by Clause 4.3 of ISO 27001, it should obtain and use the guidance in any current manual on the implementation of ISO 9001.

Note that the ISO 27001 specifications for document control (4.3.2) and record control (4.3.3) mirror those contained in ISO 9001:2008, where they are numbered 4.2.3 and 4.2.4 respectively.

13.1 Document control requirements

ISO 27001 explicitly requires the management system to be documented. Control A. 10.1.1 explicitly requires security procedures to be documented, maintained and made available to all users who need them. Other explicit documentation requirements in Annex A include:

- A.7.1.3 Acceptable use of assets
- A.8.1.1 Documented roles and responsibilities for Human Resources Security
- A.11.1.1 Access control policy
- A.15.1.1 Identification of applicable legislation.

Many of the other controls require 'formal' procedures or 'clear' communication; while these could technically be achieved without being documented, the expectation is that all processes and procedures will be.

---

11) IT Service CMM, a pocket guide, Van Haren, 2004, page 24

13.2 Contents of the ISMS documentation

Documentation has to be complete, comprehensive, in line with the requirements of the Standard and tailored to suit the needs of individual organizations. A compliant ISMS will be fully documented. ISO 27001 describes the minimum documentation that should be included in the ISMS (to meet the Standard's requirement that the organization maintains sufficient records to demonstrate compliance with the requirements of the Standard). These documents include:

- the information security policy, the scope statement for the ISMS, the risk assessment, the various control objectives, and the statement of applicability. Together, these form the ISMS policy manual
- evidence of the actions undertaken by the organization and its management to specify the scope of the ISMS (the minutes of board and steering committee meetings, as well as any specialist reports). The Standard requires that there should be records of management decisions, that all actions should be traceable to these decisions and policies, and that any results that have been recorded should be reproducible
- a description of the management framework (steering committee, etc). This could usefully be related to an organizational structure chart
- the risk treatment plan and the underpinning, documented procedures (which should include responsibilities and required actions) that implement each of the specified controls. A procedure describes who has to do what, under what conditions, or by when, and how. These procedures would be part of the policy manual which itself can be on paper or electronic. The Standard also requires that the relationship between the selected control, the results of the risk assessment and the risk treatment process, and the ISMS policy and objectives, should all be demonstrable
- the procedures that govern the management and review of the ISMS, which should include responsibilities and required actions.

Not every organization has to implement an equally complex documentation structure. The Standard notes that 'the extent of the ISMS documentation can differ from one organization to another owing to the size of the organization and the type of its activities and the scope and complexity of the security requirements and the system being managed.'[12]

---

12) ISO/IEC 27001:2005 4.3.1 note 2

13.3 Record control

The Standard's requirements around record keeping and control will be immediately familiar to anyone who already works with ISO 9001. Records have to be kept, as required by Clause 4.3.3, to provide evidence that the ISMS conforms to the requirements of the Standard. There are other records that the organization has to keep in the ordinary course of its business and these will be subject a variety of legislative and regulatory retention periods. Records that provide evidence of the effectiveness of the ISMS are of a different nature from those records that the ISMS exists to protect but, nevertheless, these records must, themselves, be controlled and must remain legible, readily identifiable and retrievable. This means that, particularly for electronic records, a means of accessing them must be retained even after hardware and software has been upgraded.

13.4 Annex A document controls

There are further document-related controls in Annex A that should be included in the document control aspects of the ISMS. They are all important controls in their own right. These controls are:

- A.7.2.1 Classification guidelines, which deal with confidentiality levels
- A.7.2.2 Information labeling and handling, which deals with how confidentiality levels are marked on information and information media
- A.15.1.3 Protection of organizational records, which deals with document retention
- A.15.1.4 Data protection and privacy of personal information.

CHAPTER 14

Management responsibility

Implementation of an ISMS is something that ISO 27001 recognizes will affect the whole organization. The requirements around scoping and the policy statement are explicit that there needs to be a documented justification for any exclusion to the scope, and that the policy should apply across the organization.

The Standard is also clear that the ISMS should be designed to meet the needs of the organization, and should be implemented and managed in a way that meets - and continues to meet - those needs.

14.1 Management direction

The Standard sets out the requirement that management 'should communicate to the organization the importance of meeting information security objectives and conforming to the information security policy.'[13] These requirements have grown stronger in successive versions of the ISMS standard as it has become ever clearer that designing and establishing an ISMS is difficult without such management support and direction.

The strategic nature of an ISMS is explicitly recognized in Clause 4.1 of the Standard, which states the requirement that the organization 'shall establish, implement, operate, monitor, review, maintain, and improve a documented ISMS within the context of the organization's overall business activities and the risks they face.' As described in Chapter 19, the organization's overall approach to risk treatment sets the context for risk assessment in line with this Standard.

Management's responsibility is so important that the whole of Clause 5 is devoted to setting out in detail the requirement that management 'shall provide evidence of its commitment to the establishment, implementation, operation, monitoring, review, maintenance and improvement of the ISMS'.

14.2 Providing evidence of management commitment

An ISO 27001 certification auditor will want to see evidence that the requirements of this clause have been met. The usual way of doing this is through a combination of

---

13) ISO/IEC 27001:2005 5.1d

interviewing the CEO or other executive who has overall responsibility for the business, as well as reviewing records (e.g. minutes, agendas and so on) of management meetings at which policies were debated and agreed, reviews carried out and improvements determined. Critically, management is required to decide 'the criteria for accepting risks and for acceptable risk levels;'[14] this is a critical step without which the risk assessment process - on which the entire ISMS development and implementation depends - cannot be carried out.

14.3 Management-related controls

There are a number of controls in Annex A that specify management involvement and which are linked to this section 5 of ISO 27001 (for a description of controls and the Statement of Applicability, see the relevant chapter in this Management Guide). These, numbered as they appear in Annex A (with quotations where necessary from the specified numbered clause), are as follows:

- A.5.1.1 Information security policy document, which must be approved by management
- A.6.1.1 Management commitment to information security; management must actively support through 'clear direction, demonstrated commitment, explicit assignment, and acknowledgement of information security responsibilities.' The key expressions of this commitment include the information security policy, the creation and empowerment of the ISO 27001 project group and how it co-ordinates information security activity (if necessary, and in line with A.6.1.2, through a management forum) and allocates information security responsibilities (A.6.1.3)
- A.6.1.4 Authorization process for information processing facilities; there must be a process for management to authorize new information processing facilities
- A.8.2.1 Management responsibilities; this control specifies that management 'shall require employees, contractors and third party users to apply security in accordance with established policies and procedures of the organization'
- A.10.1.3 Segregation of duties; this important requirement has to be taken into account when considering allocation of responsibilities
- A.11.2.4 Review of user access rights; this control requires that management 'shall review users' access rights at regular intervals using a formal process'
- A.15.1.2 Compliance with security policies and standards; this is the control that explicitly extends management responsibility through all levels of the organization,

---

14) ISO/IEC 27001:2005 5.1f

requiring managers to 'ensure that all security procedures within their area of responsibility are carried out correctly to achieve compliance with security policies and standards'.

14.4 Requirement for management review

In addition to the control requirements, the Standard mandates, at section 7 (management review of the ISMS) that management, at planned intervals, must 'review the organization's ISMS... to ensure its continuing suitability, adequacy and effectiveness.'[15] This section defines clearly the required input to the (at least annual) review process; it includes the output from all the organization's monitoring and review activity, which will is discussed in Chapter 22 of this Management Guide.

The output from the management review should be documented, and should also be implemented; it should lead to steady, ongoing and continuous improvement of the ISMS. An ISO 27001-certificated ISMS will be subject to regular certification reviews during the currency of the certificate; these reviews will focus on how the organization and its management have driven the continuous improvement process.

---

15) ISO/IEC 27001:2005

CHAPTER 15

Process approach and the PDCA cycle

The 2002 version of BS7799-2 for the first time promoted the adoption of a 'process approach' for the design and deployment of an ISMS. This approach, widely know as the 'Plan-Do-Check-Act' (PDCA) model, is familiar to quality and business managers everywhere.

The PDCA model or cycle is the Plan-Do-Check-Act cycle that was originated in the 1950s by W. Edwards Deming (figure 15.1). It states that that business processes should be treated as though they are in a continuous feedback loop so that managers can identify and change those parts of the process that need improvement. The process, or an improvement to the process, should first be planned, then implemented and its performance measured, then the measurements should be checked against the planned specification and any deviations or potential improvements identified, and reported to management for a decision about what action to take.

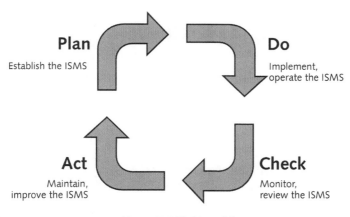

Plan
Establish the ISMS

Do
Implement, operate the ISMS

Act
Maintain, improve the ISMS

Check
Monitor, review the ISMS

Figure 15.1 *PDCA model*

15.1 PDCA and ISO 27001

ISO 27001 identifies this model in Clause 0.2 and describes how to apply it in an information security environment. Annex B to ISO 27001 (which is an informative annex, not mandatory) cross-references the OECD principles to the PDCA model. ISO 27001 'adopts the PDCA process model, which is applied to structure all ISMS processes.'[16] Application of the PDCA cycle to a process approach means that, following the basic principles of process design, there need to be both inputs to and outputs from the process. An ISMS takes as its input 'the information security requirements and expectations of the interested parties and through the necessary actions and processes produces information security outcomes that meets those requirements and expectations'.[17]

15.2 PDCA applied at the tactical level

This means that the PDCA model is applied at two levels: at the strategic level, in terms of the overall development of the ISMS itself, and at the tactical level, in terms of the development of each of the processes within the ISMS.

15.3 PDCA cycle linked to the clauses of ISO 27001

At the strategic level, the application of the PDCA cycle is applied to the development of the ISMS as described in the introduction to the Standard. The correspondence between the PDCA cycle and the stages identified in the Standard for development of the ISMS are as set out below.

Plan (Establish the ISMS, Clause 4.2.1):
• define the scope of the ISMS
• define the information security policy
• define a systematic approach to risk assessment
• carry out a risk assessment to identify, within the context of the policy and ISMS scope, the important information assets of the organization and the risks to them
• assess the risks
• identify and evaluate options for the treatment of these risks
• select, for each risk treatment decision, the control objectives and controls to be implemented
• prepare a Statement of Applicability (SoA).

---

16) ISO/IEC 27001:2005
17) Ibid

Do (Implement and operate the ISMS, Clause 4.2.2):
- formulate the risk treatment plan and its documentation, including planned processes and detailed procedures
- implement the risk treatment plan and planned controls
- provide appropriate training for affected staff, as well as awareness programmes
- manage operations and resources in line with the ISMS
- implement procedures that enable prompt detection of, and response to, security incidents.

Check (Monitor and review the ISMS, Clause 4.2.3):
- the 'check' stage has, essentially, only one step (or, set of steps): monitoring, reviewing, testing and audit.
- monitoring, reviewing, testing and audit is an ongoing process that has to cover the whole system.

Act (Maintain and improve the ISMS, Clause 4.2.4):
- testing and audit outcomes should be reviewed by management, as should the ISMS in the light of the changing risk environment, technology or other circumstances; improvements to the ISMS should be identified, documented and implemented
- thereafter, it will be subject to ongoing review, further testing and improvement implementation, a process known as 'continuous improvement'.

CHAPTER 16

Scope definition

The first planning step is the scoping exercise.

The scoping requirement is contained in Clause 4.2.1 a). The requirement is that the organization will 'define the scope and boundaries of the ISMS in terms of the characteristics of the business, the organization, its location, assets, technology, and including details of and justification for any exclusions from the scope.'

Clause 1 (Scope) of the Standard should also be read (again) at this point. It makes clear that references to 'business' anywhere in the Standard 'should be interpreted broadly to mean those activities that are core to the purposes of the organization's existence.'

Clause 1 translates into four criteria that are applied in deciding the scope of an ISMS project:

- What legal or management entity will be responsible and accountable for the ISMS?
- What information assets are owned, operated or depended upon by that entity?
- What processes are involved in manipulating, storing or sharing that information?
- What legal and regulatory requirements apply to that information (and in which jurisdictions)?

16.1 The scoping exercise

A scoping exercise should determine what is within, and what is outside, the ISMS. The ISMS will, in effect, erect a barrier between everything that is inside its perimeter and everything that is outside it. The development of the ISMS will require every point at which there is contact between the outside and the inside to be treated as a potential risk point, requiring specific and appropriate treatment.

16.2 Small organizations

In smaller organizations, everything should be within the scope of the ISMS. This is in line with the stated expectation of the Standard, which is that simple situations require simple solutions. ISO 27001's greater emphasis on the requirement that any exclusions from the scope should be specifically justified indicates an expectation that everything that is an information asset, or that has anything to do with an information asset, should be within the scope of the information security management system.

16.3 Larger organizations

In larger organizations, particularly those with multiple divisions, sites and operating units, the scoping decision is more complex. The criteria identified above enable an appropriate decision to be made. Often, the simple act of listing all the information assets and information processes helps determine clearly the scope of the ISMS. The assets that are within scope will have to be the individual subject of risk assessments, and so their early identification is advantageous to the project as a whole.

Assets, like processes, cannot be half-in and half-out of the ISMS; they are either wholly in or wholly out.

16.4 Legal and regulatory framework

The legal and regulatory framework (4.2.1. b.2) also creates a specific perspective on the scoping of the ISMS for a larger organization. Clearly, information and information management processes that are all within the scope of any one single regulation or other legal requirement must all be within the scope of the ISMS.

CHAPTER 17

Policy definition

The second planning step required by ISO 27001 is policy definition.

Clause 4.2.1.b requires the organization to define an information security policy. This requirement is also contained in the first control in Annex A, control number 5.1.1. This is the first of many clauses in ISO 27001 that are supported by the guidance and best practice of ISO 27002. Clause 5.1.1 of ISO 27002 expands on the similarly numbered Annex A requirement and matches the specification contained in Clause 4.2.1.b of ISO 27001. It explains that the control objective served by the issue of a policy document is that it provides 'management direction and support for information security in accordance with business requirements and relevant laws and regulation.'[18]

17.1 Policy and business objectives

Clause 5.1.1 goes on to state that the policy document should set a 'clear policy direction in line with business objectives'. The Standard's perspective is that a successful and useful ISMS will be one that does not undermine or block business activity. The significant risk in implementing systems that block business activity, that are not (in the language of the Standard) in line with business objectives, is that people inside the business will ignore or bypass the ISMS controls.

The information security policy is important, and must be drafted so that every word in it is clear, unambiguous and meaningful (providing a 'clear direction'). Finalization of the policy is dependent on the completion of the scoping of the project. Scoping, one of the nine steps[19] to a successful ISO 27001 implementation, makes an essential contribution to the policy definition.

The information security policy must be signed off by the board and made available as appropriate to anyone who needs it.

---

18) ISO/IEC 27001:2005

19) Nine Steps to Success: an ISO 27001 Implementation Overview (Alan Calder, ITG Publishing, 2005)

17.2 Information security governance and the ISMS

Figure 17.1 which has been adapted from the ICT governance diagram contained in ISO / IEC 38500:2008, shows how management responds to business and other pressures to direct, evaluate and monitor the effectiveness of the ISMS.

Management evaluates proposals for new (or changed) business or IT processes, in the light of prevailing risk and business requirements and, through the ISMS policy, provides risk-based direction for the organization on the controls that should be selected as part of those processes, and then monitors and evaluates the effectiveness of those controls.

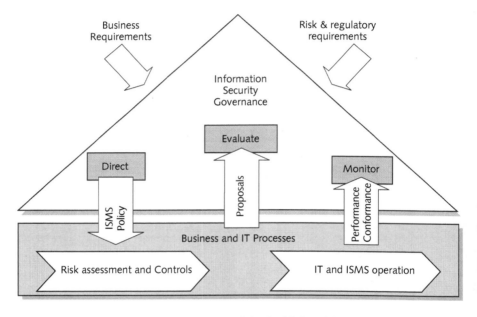

Figure 17.1 *Information security governance and the ISMS (adapted from ISO/IEC 38500:2008)*

CHAPTER 18

Risk assessment

The third planning step is risk assessment. Risk assessment is dealt with in Clauses 4.2.1.c, d, f, and g of ISO 27001, together with the supporting guidance of ISO 27002 Clause 4. This is the second area in which the two Standards are directly complementary. While ISO 27001 specifies the risk assessment steps that must be followed, ISO 27002:2005 provides further guidance, in its Clause 4, on the risk assessment process, but deliberately does not provide detailed guidance on how the individual assessment itself is to be conducted. This is because every organization is encouraged to choose the approach, which is most applicable for its industry, complexity and risk environment.

18.1 Links to other standards

In its introduction, ISO 27002:2005 describes risk assessment in terms compatible with this Management Guide and refers the reader looking for more guidance to ISO 13335-3, which contains examples of risk assessment methodologies. This guide, has now been replaced by ISO/IEC 27005:2007, which provides extensive good practice advice on the subject. ISO 27002 also adopts (from ISO Guide 73:2002) definitions of risk, risk analysis, risk assessment, risk evaluation, risk management and risk treatment. It is simplest if these definitions are adopted by any organization tackling risk management, for the sake of consistency with the Standard and commonality of approach.

18.2 Objectives of risk treatment plans

ISO 27002 states that risk treatment plans have four, linked, objectives. These are to:
- eliminate risks (terminate them)
- reduce those that cannot be eliminated to 'acceptable' levels; (treat them)
- tolerate them, exercising carefully the controls that keep them 'acceptable'
- transfer them, by means of contract or insurance, to some other organization.

The definition of what is 'acceptable' is critical to any risk treatment plan, and the Standard requires management (in Clause 5.1 f) to 'decide the criteria for accepting risks and for acceptable risk levels.' There should be evidence of the process adopted by management to make these decisions, which must fit 'within the context of the organization's overall business activities and the risks they face.'[20]

A risk treatment plan can only be drawn up once the risks have been identified, analyzed and assessed. The risk assessment process should be designed to operate within the organization's risk treatment framework and should follow the specific requirements of the Standard.

18.3 Risk assessment process

Qualitative risk assessment is by far the most widely used approach to risk analysis and is the approach expected by Clause 4.2.1.d) (Identify the risks). Numeric probability data is not required and only estimated potential loss can be used. Most qualitative risk analysis methodologies make use of a number of interrelated elements, and the Standard expects that, for each asset, its owner(s), the threat(s) to confidentiality, integrity and availability, its vulnerabilities and the impact(s) will be identified.

The Standard sets out six steps that must be followed in carrying out a risk assessment:
- identify the assets within the scope of the ISMS
- identify threats to the confidentiality, availability and integrity of those assets
- identify the vulnerabilities those threats could exploit
- assess the possible impacts of those threats
- assess the likelihood of those events occurring
- evaluate the risk.

18.4 Assets within the scope (4.2.1.d1)

The first step is to identify all the information assets (including information systems - the organization's Information Security Policy should contain a definition of this) within the scope (4.2.1.a) of the ISMS and, at the same time, to document which individual and/or department 'owns' the asset. This exercise builds on, and could be part, of the scoping exercise. The key components of this exercise are:
- identifying the boundaries (physical and logical) of what is to be protected
- identifying all the systems necessary for the reception, storage, manipulation and transmission of information or data within those boundaries and the information assets within those systems

---

20) ISO/IEC 27001:2005 4.1 General requirements

- identifying the relationships between these systems, the information assets and the organizational objectives and tasks
- identifying the systems and information assets that are critical to the achievement of these organizational objectives and tasks and, if possible, ranking them in order of priority. Clause A.7.1 is the Annex A control that deals with the asset inventory and the guidance of Clause 7.1 of ISO 17799:2005 should be taken at this point. It identifies clearly the classes or types of information asset that should be considered, and recommends that the information security classification of the asset be determined at this time - which is in line with the requirement of control A.7.2, that information should be appropriately classified.

18.5 Asset owners

At the same time as identifying the assets that are within the scope of the ISMS, the 'owners' of those assets must (4.2.1.d.1) be identified. ISO 27001 defines 'owner' as the 'individual or entity that has approved management responsibility for controlling the production, development, maintenance, use and security of the assets.'[21] Every asset must have an owner and this is contained in control requirement A.7.1.2 (ownership of assets). The owner of the asset is the person - or part of the business - who should be responsible for appropriate classification and protection of the asset.

18.6 Threats (4.2.1.d2)

These are things that can go wrong or that can 'attack' the identified assets. They can be either external or internal. This next stage, as mandated by the Standard, is to identify the potential threats to the critical systems and assets previously listed. The requirement is to identify these threats on an asset-by-asset basis. It is, of course, likely that an individual threat may appear against more than one asset but, crucially, the Standard requires the ISMS to be based on the foundation of a detailed identification and assessment of the threats to each individual information asset that is within scope. From a practical point of view, if a number of assets fall within the same class and are exactly the same (e.g. desktop computers that have the same hardware specifications, software build, connectivity configuration and user exposure), they might be considered as a class of assets and the subsequent phases of this exercise could be carried out treating them on this basis.

---

21) ISO/IEC 27001:2005 Footnote 2

18.7 Vulnerabilities (4.2.1.d3)

These leave a system open to attack by something that is classified as a threat or allow an attack to have some success or greater impact. For example, for the external threat of 'fire', a vulnerability could be the presence of inflammable materials (e.g. paper) in the server room. In the language of the Standard, a vulnerability can be exploited by a threat. The next stage in the assessment process, therefore, is to identify - for every identified asset, and for each of the threats listed alongside each of the assets, the vulnerabilities that each threat could exploit. A single asset could face a number of threats, and each threat could exploit more than one vulnerability. You need to identify them all, and one way of doing this - particularly for computer hardware and software - is to refer to standard industry sources such as Bugtraq and CVE. Any manufacturer's updates that identify vulnerabilities should be taken into account, as should the fact that not all vulnerabilities have, on any one day, yet been identified; the organization will need to be able to identify new vulnerabilities as and when they occur.

18.8 Impacts (4.2.1.d4)

The successful exploitation of a vulnerability by a threat will have an impact on the asset's availability, confidentiality or integrity. These impacts should all be identified and, wherever possible, assigned a monetary value. The Standard is clear that these impacts should be assessed under each of these three headings; a single threat, therefore, could exploit more than one vulnerability and each exploitation could have more than one type of impact.

The Standard's requirement is to assess the extent of the possible loss to the business for each potential impact. One object of this exercise is to priorities treatment (controls) and to do so in the context of the organization's acceptable risk threshold; it is acceptable to categories possible loss rather than attempt to calculate it exactly. A stepped set of financial levels should be designed, under the board's guidance, which is appropriate to the size of the organization and its current risk treatment framework. In assessing the potential costs of impact, all identifiable costs - direct, indirect and consequential - including the costs of being out of business - should be taken into account.

18.9 Risk assessment (4.2.1.e)

Practically speaking, the process until this point has been about data gathering and factual assessment. Each of the preceding stages has a relatively high degree of certainty about it. The vulnerabilities should be capable of technical, logical or physical identification. The decisions that have to be made are those that relate to the actions the organization will take to counter those threats. This means that the actual risks have now to be assessed and related to the organization's overall 'risk appetite' - that is, the organization's willingness to take on risk. Risk assessment involves identifying the potential business harm that might result from each of the identified risks.

18.10 Likelihood

Until this point, the assessment has been carried out as though there was an equal likelihood of every identified threat actually happening. This is not really the case and this is therefore where there must be an assessment of the likelihood or probability of the impact actually occurring. Probabilities might range from 'not very likely' (e.g., major earthquake in Southern England destroying primary and backup facilities) to 'almost daily' (e.g. several hundred automated malware and hack attacks against the network).

18.11 Calculate the risk level

The final step in this exercise is to assess the risk level for each impact and to transfer the details to the corporate asset and risk log. Risk level is a function of impact and probability. Three levels of risk assessment are usually adequate: low, moderate and high. Where the likely impact is low and the probability is also low, then the risk level could be considered low. Where the impact is at least high and the probability is also at least high, then the risk level would be high; anything between these two measures would be classed as moderate. However, every organization has to decide for itself what it wants to set as the thresholds for categorizing each potential impact.

CHAPTER 19

Risk treatment plan

Clause 4.2.2.a of ISO 27001 (supported by Clause 4.2 of ISO 27002) requires the organization to 'formulate a risk treatment plan that identifies the appropriate management action, responsibilities and priorities for managing information security risks'. This clause also specifically cross-refers to Clause 5, a substantial clause dealing in detail with management responsibility, and which was covered earlier in this Management Guide. The risk treatment plan must be documented. It should be set within the context of the organization's information security policy and it should clearly identify the organization's approach to risk and its criteria for accepting risk. These criteria should, where a risk treatment framework already exists, be consistent with the requirements of the Standard.

The Standard requires (4.2.2.a and Clause 5) that the risk treatment plan is formally defined and described, that it should contain prioritized information security actions, and that the responsibilities for carrying it out, reviewing it and renewing it, should be formally allocated.

19.1 Documenting the risk treatment plan

At the heart of the risk treatment plan is a detailed schedule, which shows, for each identified risk, how the organization has decided to treat it, what controls are already in place, what additional controls are considered necessary, and the timeframe for implementing them. The acceptable level of risk needs to be identified for each risk, as well as the risk treatment option that will bring the risk within an acceptable level.

The risk treatment plan links the risk assessment (detailed, as described in the previous chapter, in the corporate information asset and risk log) to the identification and design of appropriate controls, as described in the Statement of Applicability, such that the board-defined approach to risk is implemented, tested and improved. This plan should also ensure that there is adequate funding (4.2.2.b) and resources (4.2.2.a) for implementation of the selected controls and should set out clearly what these are.

The risk treatment plan should also identify the individual competence and broader training and awareness (4.2.2.e) requirements necessary for its execution and continuous improvement.

19.2 Risk treatment plan and PDCA approach

The risk treatment plan is the key document that links all four phases of the PDCA cycle for the ISMS. It is a high-level, documented identification of who is responsible for delivering which risk management objectives, of how this is to be done, with what resources, and how this is to be assessed and improved.

CHAPTER 20

The Statement of Applicability

While the Statement of Applicability is central to an ISMS and to accredited certification of the ISMS (it is the document from which an auditor will begin the process of confirming whether or not appropriate controls are in place and operative), it can really only be prepared once the risk assessment has been completed and the risk treatment plan documented.

The Statement of Applicability is a statement as to which of the controls identified in Annex A to ISO 27001 are applicable to the organization, and which are not. It can also, and in addition, contain controls selected from other sources.

20.1 Controls and Annex A

The Standard, at Clause 4.2.1.g, requires the organization to select appropriate control objectives and controls from those specified in Annex A of ISO 27001 (which 'have been found to be commonly relevant in organizations'), and requires the selection (and exclusion) of controls to be justified . However, it clearly invites organizations to approach this task exhaustively and states that additional controls may also be selected from other sources.

ISO 27002 provides good practice on the purpose and implementation of each of the controls listed in Annex A. There are, however, some areas in which organizations may need to go further than is specified in ISO 27002; the extent to which this may be necessary is driven by the extent to which technology and threats have evolved since the finalization of ISO 27002:2005.

20.2 Controls (4.2.1.f.1)

Controls are the countermeasures for vulnerabilities. The formal ISO 27002:2005 definition is a 'means of managing risk, including policies, procedures, guidelines, practices or organizational structures, which can be of an administrative, technical, management, or legal nature. Control is also used as a synonym for safeguard or countermeasure'.

Apart from knowingly accepting risks that fall within whatever criteria of acceptability the organization adopted in its risk treatment plan, or transferring the risk (through contract or insurance), the organization can decide to implement a control to reduce the risk.

20.3 Residual risks

It is not possible or practical to provide total security against every single risk, but it is possible to provide effective security against most risks by controlling them to a level where the residual risk is acceptable to management. Management must formally accept the residual risk (Clause 4.2.1.h).

Risks can and do change, however, so the process of reviewing and assessing risks and controls is an essential, ongoing one (Clause 4.2.3).

20.4 Control objectives

Controls are selected in the light of a control objective. A control objective is a statement of an organization's intent to control some part of its processes or assets and what it intends to achieve through application of the control. One control objective may be served by a number of controls.

Annex A of ISO 27001 identifies appropriate control objectives and lists, for each of the control objectives, the controls which at a minimum serve those objectives. The organization must select its control objectives from Annex A in the light of its risk assessment, and then ensure that the controls it chooses to implement (whether from the Annex or from additional sources) will enable it to achieve the identified objective.

20.5 Plan for security incidents

It is important that, when considering controls, the likely security incidents that may need to be detected are identified, considered and planned for. Clause 4.2.2.h of the Standard requires the implementation of controls that will enable 'prompt detection of and response to security incidents'. In effect, the process of selecting individual controls from those listed in the Standard's Annex A should include consideration of what evidence will be required, and what measurements of effectiveness (4.2.2.d) will be made to demonstrate that:

- the control has been implemented and is working effectively
- each risk has, thereby, been reduced to an acceptable level, as required by Clause 4.2.1 of the Standard. Controls must be constructed in such a manner that any error,

or failure during its execution, is capable of prompt detection and that planned corrective action, whether automated or manual, is effective in reducing the risk of whatever may happen next to an acceptable level.

CHAPTER 21

Do - implement and operate the ISMS

The first phase of implementing an ISMS concludes, according to ISO 27001, with the completion of the Statement of Applicability. This SoA must identify the control objectives and controls selected and the reasons for their selection, which points backwards to the risk assessment and the risk treatment criteria selected in the risk treatment plan. The Standard also requires an identification of the controls currently implemented (4.2.2.j.2) and the vast majority of the controls identified in Annex A relate to the day-to-day operation of the ISMS.

This enables the organization to put together the second and most important part of the risk treatment plan, the 'management action, resources, responsibilities and priorities for managing information security risks,'[22] which is the detailed set of actions that, between them, enable the organization to actually implement its ISMS. As described earlier, the risk treatment plan is the key document that links all four phases of the PDCA cycle for the ISMS and which ensures that everything that needs to be done is actually done.

21.1 Implementation

The rest of this second phase of the ISMS design and implementation involves the following five activities:
- implement the risk treatment plan and the controls identified in the SoA (4.2.2.b and c)
- define how to measure and assess the effectiveness of all the controls (4.2.2.d)
- implement training and awareness programmes (4.2.2.e), which links to control A.8.2.2, information security awareness, education and training
- manage the ISMS (4.2.2.f and g). All the interlocking controls and processes must be kept working, new threats identified, evaluated and, if necessary, neutralized. People must be recruited and trained, their performance supervised, and their skills developed in line with the changing needs of the business. The effectiveness of the ISMS must be managed and its long term, continuous improvement planned and led
- implement an incident detection and response procedure (4.2.2.h), the overall importance of which is indicated by the fact that it links to a clause that was

22) ISO/IEC 27001:2005 4.2.2.a

introduced, for the first time at the highest level, in ISO 27002:2005, which is Clause 13, information security incident management. This clause contains two control objectives and five controls that differentiate between an event and an incident and which define how the response should be managed.

CHAPTER 22

Check - monitor and review the ISMS

Clause 4.2.3 of the Standard is all about monitoring and review. It reflects strongly the requirement that management is actively involved in the long-term management of the ISMS while recognizing the reality that the information security threat environment changes even more quickly than the business environment. This clause deals, broadly, with three types of activity: monitoring, auditing and reviewing.

22.1 Monitoring

The purpose of monitoring activity is primarily to detect processing errors and information security events quickly so that immediate corrective action can be taken. Monitoring should be formal, systematic and widespread. Security category A.10.10, Monitoring, contains controls that are specifically related to monitoring IT activity and these are linked to this part of ISO 27001. Control area A.13, information security incident management, also has at its heart the notion that the organization must monitor for deviations and incidents, respond to them and learn from them.

22.2 Auditing

Audits, on the other hand, are specifically designed and planned to ensure that the controls documented in the SoA are effective and being applied, and to identify non-conformances and opportunities for improvement. Control objective A15.2 (Compliance with security policies and standards, and technical compliance checking) deals specifically with this issue and mandates regular, planned compliance reviews at both the process and the technical levels. A.15.3 deals with the security requirements for audit tools. The audit requirement is described in more depth in Clause 6 of ISO 27001, which lays out two important aspects of the process:

- the audit programme 'shall be planned, taking into consideration the status and importance of the processes and areas to be audited, as well as the results of previous audits'[23]

---

23) ISO/IEC 27001:2005 clause 6

- 'the management responsible for the area being audited shall ensure that actions are taken without undue delay to eliminate detected non-conformities and their causes'.[24]

Again, the Standard is clear that management at all levels of the organization has a role to play in the effective implementation, maintenance and improvement of the ISMS. This must be taken into account in managerial and supervisory job descriptions, employment contracts, induction and other training, and performance reviews.

22.3 Reviewing

Reviews of internal and external audits policies, performance reports, exception reports, risk assessment reports and all the associated policies and procedures are undertaken to ensure that the ISMS is continuing to be effective within its changing context.
There is, of course, a close interaction between the three elements of this stage and a number of the controls in Annex A and ISO 27002. The Annex A controls that are directly relevant to this stage of the ISMS PDCA cycle are:

- A.5.1.2 Review of the Information Security Policy
- A.5.1.8 Independent review of information security
- A.10.2.2 Monitoring and review of third party services
- A.10.10 'Monitoring' is itself a single control objective that is related, obviously, to monitoring, and which contains six controls
- A.11.2.4 Review of user access rights
- A.12.2 Correct processing in applications, is a control objective that in effect deals with monitoring application use and data processing
- A.13.2.2 Learning from information security incidents
- A.14.1.5 Testing, maintaining and re-assessing business continuity plans.

All these controls must be addressed in this third phase of the ISMS development and implementation. The findings and outcomes of the monitoring and reporting activity must be translated into corrective or improvement action and, for the purposes of the ISMS, the audit trail that demonstrates the decision making process and the implementation of those decisions should be retained in the ISMS records.

---

24) ISO/IEC 27001:2005, Clause 6

CHAPTER 23

Act - maintain and improve the ISMS

This is a short chapter, and it reflects the relative brevity of the requirements of section 4.2.4 of ISO 27001. This clause sets out the requirement that everything learned through the monitoring and reviewing activity discussed in the previous chapter should be implemented. It also links to section 8 of the Standard, whose three clauses (8.1, continual improvement; 8.2, corrective action and 8.3, preventative action) specify the nature and purpose of the activity that must be part and parcel of the day-to-day activity of everyone involved in the day-to-day management of the ISMS.

23.1 Management review

In this context, this section also links to section 7 (and control A.5.1.2), which deals with management review of the ISMS, and which stresses that this management review should take into account the 'status of preventative and corrective actions,'[25] as well as any changes anywhere or to anything that might affect the ISMS, and recommendations for improvement.

It should be noted that corrective and preventative action should be prioritized on the basis of a risk assessment.[26]

ISO 27001 also calls, at control A.5.1.8, for an 'independent review of information security', which should take place at planned intervals (or whenever there have been significant changes), and should be comprehensive ('control objectives, controls, policies, processes, and procedures'). Third party certification would meet this control requirement.

Assessing and evaluating risks is a core competence required in any organization that is serious about achieving and maintaining ISO 27001 accredited certification. The final sentence of the Standard, which makes the point that the prevention 'of non-conformities is often more cost-effective than corrective action,' sums up the risk-based, cost-effective, common-sense approach of the Standard.

---

25) ISO/IEC 27001:2005 7.2.d
26) IOS/IEC 27001:2005 8.3

CHAPTER 24

ISO 27001:2005 Annex A

ISO 27001:2005 Annex A has 11 major clauses or control areas numbered from A.5 to A.15, each of which identifies one or more control objectives. Each control objective is served by one or more controls. Every control is sequentially numbered.

There are, in total, 133 sub clauses, each of which has a four-character alphanumeric clause number.

Each of these sub-clauses is an ISO 27001 control and each of them needs to be considered and a decision made as to whether or not it is applicable within the organization's ISMS. As the controls are selected, the statement of applicability (SoA) can be drawn up. This SoA, specified in 4.2.1.j of the Standard, is documentation of the decisions reached against the requirement to consider controls and is also an explanation or justification of why any controls that are listed in Annex A have not been selected.

24.1 SoA and external parties

This document must be reviewed on a defined, regular basis. It is the document that is used to demonstrate to third parties the degree of security that has been implemented and is usually referred to, with its issue status, in the certificate of compliance issued by third party certification bodies.

24.2 Annex A clauses

Annex A is aligned with ISO 27002:2005; this means that precisely the same control objectives, controls, clause numbering and wording are used in both Annex A and in ISO 27002. ISO 27002, however, provides substantial, detailed, technology-neutral and vendor-independent guidance on how to implement each of the controls and it is therefore an essential component of an ISO 27001 implementation. Note the clear statement that 'the lists in these tables are not exhaustive and an organization may consider that additional control objectives and controls are necessary.'[27] The 11 control clauses of Annex A (it does not have clauses 1 - 4) all start with an A and are listed hereafter.

---

27) ISO/IEC 27001:2005 Annax A Introduction

- A5: Security policy
- A6: Organizing information security
- A7: Asset management
- A8: Human resources security
- A9: Physical and environmental security
- A10: Communications and operations management
- A11: Access control
- A12: Information systems acquisition, development and maintenance
- A13: Information security incident management
- A14: Business continuity management
- A15: Compliance

CHAPTER 25

Annex A control areas and controls

Each of the clauses of Annex A deals with one or more security categories, and each security category has a control objective and one or more controls that will serve to secure that objective. The clauses, security categories, control objectives and controls are as follows.

25.1 Clause A5: Security policy

5.1   **Information security policy**: to provide management direction and support for information security in accordance with business requirements and relevant laws and regulations

5.1.1   Information security policy document

5.1.2   Review of the information security policy

25.2 Clause A6: Organization of information security

6.1   **Internal organization**: to manage information security within the organization

6.1.1   Management commitment to information security

6.1.2   Information security co-ordination

6.1.3   Allocation of information security responsibilities

6.1.4   Authorization process for information processing facilities

6.1.5   Confidentiality agreements

6.1.6   Contact with authorities

6.1.7   Contact with special interest groups

6.1.8   Independent review of information security

6.2   **External Parties**: to maintain the security of organizational information processing facilities and information assets accessed, processed, communicated to or managed by external parties

6.2.1   Identification of risks related to external parties

6.2.2   Addressing security when dealing with customers

6.2.3   Addressing security in third party agreements

25.3 Clause A7: Asset management

7.1   **Responsibility for assets**: to achieve and maintain appropriate protection of organizational assets

7.1.1   Inventory of assets

7.1.2   Ownership of assets

7.1.3   Acceptable use of assets

7.2   **Information classification**: to ensure that information assets receive an appropriate level of protection

7.2.1   Classification guidelines

7.2.2   Information labeling and handling

25.4 Clause A8: Human resources security

8.1   **Before employment**: to ensure that all employees, contractors and third party users understand their responsibilities, and are suitable for the roles they are considered for, and to reduce the risk of theft, fraud or misuse of facilities

8.1.1   Roles and responsibilities

8.1.2   Screening

8.1.3   Terms and conditions of employment

8.2   **During employment**: to ensure that all employees, contractors and third party users are aware of information security threats and concerns, their responsibilities and liabilities, and are equipped to support organizational security policy in the course of their normal work, and to reduce the risk of human error.

8.2.1   Management responsibilities

8.2.2   Information security awareness, education and training

8.2.3   Disciplinary process

8.3   **Termination or change of employment**: to ensure that employees, contractors and third party users exit an organization or change employment in an orderly manner

8.3.1   Termination responsibilities

8.3.2   Return of assets

8.3.3   Removal of access rights

25.5 Clause A9: Physical and environmental security

9.1   **Secure areas**: to prevent unauthorized physical access, damage and
        interference to the organization's premises and information
9.1.1   Physical security perimeter
9.1.2   Physical entry controls
9.1.3   Securing offices, rooms and facilities
9.1.4   Protecting against external and environmental threats
9.1.5   Working in secure areas
9.1.6   Public access, delivery and loading areas

9.2   **Equipment security**: to prevent loss, damage, theft or compromise of assets
        and interruption to the organization's activities
9.2.1   Equipment siting and protection
9.2.2   Supporting utilities
9.2.3   Cabling security
9.2.4   Equipment maintenance
9.2.5   Security of equipment off-premises
9.2.6   Secure disposal or re-use of equipment
9.2.7   Removal of property

25.6 Clause A10: Communications and operations management

10.1   **Operational procedures and responsibilities**: to ensure the correct and
         secure operation of information processing facilities
10.1.1   Documented operating procedures
10.1.2   Change management
10.1.3   Segregation of duties
10.1.4   Separation of development, test and operational facilities

10.2   **Third party service delivery management**: To implement and maintain the
         appropriate level of information security and service delivery in line with
         third party service delivery agreements
10.2.1   Service delivery
10.2.2   Monitoring and review of third party services
10.2.3   Managing changes to third party services

10.3   **System planning and acceptance**: to minimize the risks of systems failures

10.3.1   Capacity planning

10.3.2   System acceptance

10.4   **Protection against malicious and mobile code**: to protect the integrity of software and information

10.4.1   Controls against malicious code

10.4.2   Controls against mobile code

10.5   **Back-up**: to maintain the integrity and availability of information and information processing facilities

10.5.1   Information back-up

10.6   **Network security management**: to ensure the safeguarding of information in networks and the protection of the supporting infrastructure

10.6.1   Network controls

10.6.2   Security of network services

10.7   **Media handling**: to prevent the unauthorized disclosure, modification, removal or destruction of assets and interruption to business activities

10.7.1   Management of removable computer media

10.7.2   Disposal of media

10.7.3   Information handling procedures

10.7.4   Security of system documentation

10.8   **Exchanges of information**: to maintain the security of information exchanged within an organization and with any external entity

10.8.1   Information exchange policies and procedures

10.8.2   Exchange agreements

10.8.3   Physical media in transit

10.8.4   Electronic messaging

10.8.5   Business information systems

10.9   **Electronic commerce services**: to ensure the security of electronic commerce services, and their secure use

10.9.1   Electronic commerce

10.9.2   On-line transactions

10.9.3   Publicly available systems

10.10   **Monitoring**: to detect unauthorized activities
10.10.1 Audit logging
10.10.2 Monitoring system use
10.10.3 Protection of log information
10.10.4 Administrator and operator logs
10.10.5 Fault logging
10.10.6 Clock synchronization

25.7 Clause A11: Access control

11.1   **Business requirement for access control**: to control access to information
11.1.1   Access control policy

11.2   **User access management**: to ensure authorized users' access and to prevent unauthorized access to information systems
11.2.1   User registration
11.2.2   Privilege management
11.2.3   User password management
11.2.4   Review of user access rights

11.3   **User responsibilities**: to prevent unauthorized user access, and compromise or theft of information and information processing facilities
11.3.1   Password use
11.3.2   Unattended user equipment
11.3.3   Clear desk and clear screen policy

11.4   **Network access control**: to protect networked services from unauthorized access
11.4.1   Policy on use of network services
11.4.2   User authentication for external connections
11.4.3   Equipment identification in the network
11.4.4   Remote diagnostic and configuration port protection
11.4.5   Segregation in networks
11.4.6   Network connection control
11.4.7   Network routing control

11.5   **Operating system access control**: to prevent unauthorized access to information systems

11.5.1   Secure log-on procedures
11.5.2   User identification and authentication
11.5.3   Password management system
11.5.4   Use of system utilities
11.5.5   Session time-out
11.5.6   Limitation of connection time

11.6   **Application and information access control**: to prevent unauthorized access to information held in information systems
11.6.1   Information access restriction
11.6.2   Sensitive system isolation

11.7   **Mobile computing and teleworking**: to ensure information security when using mobile computing and teleworking facilities
11.7.1   Mobile computing and communications
11.7.2   Teleworking

25.8 Clause A12: Information systems acquisition, development and maintenance

12.1   **Security requirements of information systems**: to ensure that security is an integral party of information systems
12.1.1   Security requirements analysis and specification

12.2   **Correct processing in applications**: to prevent errors, loss, unauthorized modification or misuse of information in applications
12.2.1   Input data validation
12.2.2   Control of internal processing
12.2.3   Message integrity
12.2.4   Output data validation

12.3   **Cryptographic controls**: to protect the confidentiality, authenticity or integrity of information by cryptographic means
12.3.1   Policy on the use of cryptographic controls
12.3.2   Key Management

12.4   **Security of system files**: to ensure the security of system files
12.4.1   Control of operational software

12.4.2   Protection of system test data

12.4.3   Access control to program source code

12.5   **Security in development and support processes**: to maintain the security of application system software and information

12.5.1   Change control procedures

12.5.2   Technical review of applications after operating system changes

12.5.3   Restrictions on changes to software packages

12.5.4   Information leakage

12.5.5   Outsourced software development

12.6   **Technical vulnerability management**: to prevent the damage resulting from exploitation of published vulnerabilities

12.6.1   Control of technical vulnerabilities

25.9 Clause A13: Information security incident management

13.1   **Reporting information security events and weaknesses**: to ensure information security events and weaknesses associated with information systems are communicated in a manner allowing timely corrective action to be taken

13.1.1   Reporting information security events

13.1.2   Reporting security weaknesses

13.2   **Management of information security incidents and improvements**: to ensure a consistent and effective approach is applied to the management of information security incidents

13.2.1   Responsibilities and procedures

13.2.2   Learning from information security incidents

13.2.3   Collection of evidence

25.10 Clause A14: Business continuity management

14.1   **Information security aspects of business continuity management**: to counteract interruptions to business activities, to protect critical business processes from the effects of major failures or disasters and to ensure their timely resumption

14.1.1   Including information security in the business continuity management process
14.1.2   Business continuity and risk assessment
14.1.3   Developing and implementing continuity plans including information security
14.1.4   Business continuity planning framework
14.1.5   Testing, maintaining and re-assessing business continuity plans

25.11 Clause A15: Compliance

15.1   **Compliance with legal requirements**: to avoid breaches of any law, statutory, regulatory or contractual obligations, and of any security requirements
15.1.1   Identification of applicable legislation
15.1.2   Intellectual property rights (IPR)
15.1.3   Protection of organizational records
15.1.4   Data protection and privacy of personal information
15.1.5   Prevention of misuse of information processing facilities
15.1.6   Regulation of cryptographic controls

15.2   **Compliance with security policies and standards and technical compliance**: to ensure compliance of systems with organizational security policies and standards
15.2.1   Compliance with security policy and standards
15.2.2   Technical compliance checking

15.3   **Information systems audit considerations**: to maximize the effectiveness of and to minimize interference to/from the information systems audit process
15.3.1   Information systems audit controls
15.3.2   Protection of information systems audit controls

26 ISO 27001 and CobiT

CobiT, or Control Objectives for Information and related Technology, is 'a model for the control of the IT environment.'[28] While this book is not about CobiT, anyone deploying an ISO 27001 ISMS should be aware of it and so this is a brief introduction that contextualizes CobiT's value in the design and development of an ISMS to meet the requirements of ISO 27001.

26.1 Background to CobiT

CobiT was first published in 1996, and has been revised three times, with the most recent version - CobiT 4.1 - being published in 2007. It was originally developed by the research institute of ISACA (the Information Systems Audit and Control Association) after 1994. That research institute became the IT Governance Institute in 2003. Its background is in information systems audit and CobiT was originally developed by IT auditors primarily for use by auditors. It has expanded and evolved to become a framework for the broader control of the IT environment.

26.2 CobiT framework

The CobiT framework consists of four domains and 34 processes. The four CobiT domains are:
- plan and organize (PO)
- acquire and implement (AI)
- deliver and support (DS)
- monitor and evaluate (ME)

These domains do not map to the PDCA cycle of ISO 27001, even though there may at first appear to be a similarity in the diagrammatic representations of the four CobiT domains and the PDCA cycle.
'A powerful and central theme in CobiT is the focus on IT processes.'[29] It is this focus,

---

28) IT Governance based on CobiT: a Pocket Guide, van Haren 2004, page 35
29) Ibid, page 70

allied to the fact that CobiT processes are developed within a framework that uses the concepts of 'control objective' and 'control' in a way that will be familiar to anyone implementing an ISO 27001 ISMS, that makes CobiT so useful for an ISMS implementation.

26.3 CobiT process DS5

One CobiT process, DS5, ensure systems security, looks as though it contains the requirements of ISO 27001. It does not ; it maps to some of the controls and management system requirements of ISO 27001 but is not a substitute for the Standard. The key activities of DS5 are:
* to define and manage an IT Security Plan
* to define, establish and operate an identify management process
* to monitor potential and actual security incidents
* to periodically review and validate user access rights and privileges
* to establish and maintain procedures for maintaining and safeguarding crypographic keys
* to implement and maintain technical and procedural controls to protect information flows across networks, to conduct regular vulnerability assesments.

There are a number of critical ISO 27001 processes missing from DS5, the most obvious and important of which are:
* risk assessment (although this is touched on in CobiT PO9)
* management direction
* management review.

Application of DS5 alone will not enable an organization to prepare for ISO 27001 certification.

26.4 Gaps and overlaps

At a higher level, while there is no one-to-one mapping between CobiT processes and ISO 27001 processes, there are areas of significant overlap and each has different strengths. Each also has significant weaknesses. CobiT, for instance, does not include business continuity management, which is a fundamental process for organizational survival.

Many of the control objectives and controls that are identified in ISO 27001 Annex A are also identified in individual CobiT processes. This raises the possibility that deployment of CobiT processes might, in some cases, be an appropriate method of achieving an ISO 27001 control objective.

All this has led a number of organizations to combine the two frameworks, using ISO 27001 to deal more specifically with information security issues and CobiT to deal with broader IT management issues.

CobiT processes such as PO1 (Define a strategic IT plan), PO2 (Define the information architecture) and PO3 (Determine technological direction) are critical precursors to any attempt to design and develop an ISMS that is in line with the business requirements. Table 26.1 shows a mapping between ISO 27001 processes and those in CobiT.

ISO 27001 processes	CobiT processes
4.2.1.a & b Define ISMS scope and policy	PO6 Communicate management aims and direction
4.2.1.c et seq Risk assessment	PO9 Assess and manage IT risks
4.2.2.e and 5.2.2. Training and awareness	DS7 Educate and train users
4.2.2.f Manage operations	DS13 Manage operations
4.2.2.h & 8 Security incidents and continuous improvement	DS10 Manage problems and incidents
4.2.3 Monitor and review	ME1 Monitor & evaluate IT performance & ME2 Monitor & evaluate internal control
4.3 Documentation requirements	PO6 Communicate management aims and direction
6 Internal ISMS audits	ME2 Monitor & evaluate internal control

Table 26.1 *Mapping processes ISO 27001 and CobiT*

There are also a number of ISO 27001 Annex A controls that can be met using processes that are mapped in CobiT. These include, for example, controls in A.10.2, which relate to third party service delivery management and CobiT's DS2, Manage third party services, which is obviously relevant, just as DS3, Manage performance and capacity is obviously relevant to ISO 27001's capacity management.

Anyone who wishes to pursue CobiT in more detail should obtain copies of the detailed CobiT documentation.

CHAPTER 27

ISO 27001, ITIL and ISO 20000

ISO 27001 recognizes that today's business services are increasingly delivered or enabled using information technology. Business and IT management need guidance and support on how to manage the IT infrastructure in order to cost-effectively improve functionality and quality. IT Service Management (ITSM) is a concept that deals with how to define and deliver that guidance and support. This IT service concept views IT from an end user perspective i.e. IT service is what the customer or consumer receives. The IT service itself can be made up of hardware, software and communication facilities, but is perceived by the customer/consumer as a self contained, coherent entity.

27.1 ITIL

ITIL (the IT Infrastructure Library) is a set of best practices at the heart of IT service management. It provides guidance on how to manage IT infrastructure so as to streamline IT services in line with business expectations. ITIL is a best practice framework, presenting the consolidated experience of organizations worldwide on how best to manage IT services to meet business expectations.

ITIL defines the organizational structure and skill requirements of an IT area and documents a set of operational management procedures to allow management of an IT operation and infrastructure. Importantly, the operational procedures are supplier independent and technology-neutral.

27.2 Background to ITIL

ITIL was originally developed during the 1980s by the UK's Central Computer and Telecommunication Agency (CCTA), who created ITIL (version 1) as an approach independent of vendor technology and caters to organizations with differing technical and business needs. CCTA has now become part of the Office of Government Commerce (OGC) who, as the official publisher of ITIL, updated it and published version 2. This was followed, in summer 2007, by ITIL version 3. ITIL has been widely adopted across the world, in both the public and the private sector, and is now recognized as best practice for IT service management and is deployed in organizations of all sizes.

27.3 BS15000/ISO 20000

ISO/IEC 20000 is a two-part standard that specifies best practice for IT service management, and is the specification for IT service management against which an organization's actual practices can be certified.

Logically, any organization that is implementing ISO 27001 might look to ITIL to provide best practice guidance in developing operational management procedures in any area that might fall under a service management heading. Any organization that has a substantial service management component might additionally expect that component to achieve ISO 20000 certification or, if it depends on an external supplier for IT services, it might expect that supplier to achieve both ISO 27001 and ISO 20000.

27.4 ITIL Security Management

ITILv2 included one manual titled 'Best Practice for Security Management', which was written and published in 1999. There is no updated equivalent in ITILv3. This manual aligns with BS7799:1995, although it also took BS7799:1999 (draft) into account. This means that it was written before the publication of BS7799 as a two-part standard and is aligned with what is now ISO 27002, although the version with which it is aligned has now been updated twice.

This manual's starting point is existing ITIL processes, to which it then adds security processes. Although it is technically out-of-date, it still supplies useful guidance to any organization that treats any part of its IT operation as a 'service', particularly if that service is the subject of an SLA (Service Level Agreement), whether internal or external.

27.5 ISO 27001, ITIL and CobiT

ITIL processes are not templates that can simply be forced onto an organization. They need to be selected, adapted and suited to each individual organization. In organizations that have the time to create an IT management infrastructure that is truly best in class, ISO 27001, ITIL and CobiT are likely to be combined in a way that ensures IT really delivers business goals and performance.

Bibliography of related standards and guides

Both ISO 27001 and ISO 27002 include extensive bibliographies of standards that may be relevant to the Standard. Those lists are not repeated here. The essential documents, without which no-one should attempt an ISMS implementation, and which should be available online through national standards bodies and other licensed distributors are:

- ISO/IEC 27001:2005 Information technology - security techniques - information security management systems - requirements
- ISO/IEC 27002:2005 Information technology - security techniques - Code of practice for information security management

The following documents are all identified as being helpful, but are not mandatory:

- ISO/IEC 20000-1:2005 IT Service management - specification for service management
- ISO/IEC 20000-2:2005 IT Service Management - code of practice for service management
- BS25999-1:2006 - code of practice for business continuity management
- BS25999-2:2007 - specification for business continuity management
- ITILv3 Complete Lifecycle Publication Suite
- ISO 9001:2008 Quality management systems - requirements
- CobiT (version 4.1)

Accredited certification and other bodies

United Kingdom Accreditation Service: ....www.ukas.com

Quality Register at TSO:.. www.quality-register.co.uk

Institute for Internal Auditors:... www.theiia.org/itaudit

Institute of Quality Assurance:... www.iqa.org

International Accreditation Forum:.. www.iaf.nu

International Auditor and Training Certification Association: .... www.iatca.org

International Register of Certificated Auditors: .... www.irca.org

International Standards Organization: .... www.iso.ch

BSI: ....www.bsi-global.com

Bureau Veritas Quality International (BVQI): .... www.bvqi.com

DNV Certification Ltd:...www.dnv.com

Lloyd's Register Quality Assurance Ltd (LRQA): ....www.lrqa.com/

National Quality Assurance Ltd (NQA):.. www.nqa.com

SGS Yarsley: .... www.sgs.com

Information assurance (UK public sector):...................... www.cabinetoffice.gov.uk/csia

Other leading ITSM Books

84743149R00057

Made in the USA
Middletown, DE
21 August 2018